VOLCANOES

www.worldbook.com

World Book, Inc.
180 N. LaSalle Street, Suite 900
Chicago, IL 60601
USA

For information about other World Book publications, visit our website at
http://www.worldbook.com or call **1-800-WORLDBK (967-5325).**

For information about sales to schools and libraries, call
1-800-975-3250 (United States); 1-800-837-5365 (Canada).

3rd edition

Library of Congress Cataloging-in-Publication Data

Title: Volcanoes.
Description: 3rd edition. | Chicago, IL: World Book, Inc., [2018] | Series: World Book's library of natural disasters | Includes index.
Identifiers: LCCN 2017054269
ISBN 9780716699422 (hc.) | ISBN 9780716694885 (pf.)
Subjects: LCSH: Volcanoes--Juvenile literature.
Classification: LCC QE521.3 .V6425 2018 | DDC 363.34/95--dc23 LC record available at https://lccn.loc.gov/2017054269

Set: ISBN: 978-0-7166-9928-6 (hc.)

Editor in Chief: Paul A. Kobasa

Print Content Development

Director: Tom Evans
Managing Editor: Jeff De La Rosa

Editors: William D. Adams, Nicholas Kilzer

Researcher: Jacqueline Jasek

Manager, Contracts & Compliance (Rights & Permissions): Loranne K. Shields

Manager, Indexing Services: David Pofelski

Graphics and Design

Coordinator, Design Development and Production: Brenda B. Tropinski
Senior Visual Communications Designer: Melanie Bender
Media Editor: Rosalia Bledsoe
Senior Cartographer: John M. Rejba

Production

Manufacturing Manager: Anne Fritzinger
Proofreader: Nathalie Strassheim

Product development:
Arcturus Publishing Limited

Writer: Chris Oxlade
Editors: Nicola Barber, Alex Woolf
Designer: Jane Hawkins
Illustrator: Stefan Chabluk

Acknowledgments:

All maps and illustrations were prepared by the World Book staff unless otherwise noted.

Corbis: 10, 15, 37 (Reuters), 12 (Jim Sugar), 13 (Robert Holmes), 16 (Gary Braasch), 18 (Imelda Medina/ epa), 19, 24, 49 (Roger Ressmeyer), 25 (Earl & Nazima Kowall), 34, 45 (Corbis), 35 (Rykoff Collection), 36 (Yann Arthus-Bertrand), 38, 39 (Jacques Langevin/ Corbis Sygma), 47, 50 (Bettmann), 48 (Jeremy Bembaron/ Corbis Sygma).

Getty Images: cover (Pétur Reynisson), 20 (Three Lions), 23 (Bettmann), 28 (Claudio Santana/ AFP), 29 (Ivan Konar/ LAtinContent).

NASA: 26 (GSFC/ Jeff Schmaltz/ MODIS Land Rapid Response Team).

Science Photo Library: 8 (Prof. Stewart Lowther), 9 (Alan Sirulnikoff), 11, 30 (Bernhard Edmaier), 17 (Jack Fields), 31, 32, 33 (Science Photo Library), 40 (Robert M Carey, NOAA), 41 (Gary Hincks), 46 (NASA).

Shutterstock: 5 (Bychkov Kirill Alexandrovich), 22 (Chad Zuber), 27 (Johann Helgason), 43 (Todd Mestemacher).

TABLE OF CONTENTS

Glossary There is a glossary of terms on pages 53-54. Terms defined in the glossary are in type **that looks like this** on their first appearance on any spread (two facing pages).

Additional resources Books for further reading and recommended websites are listed on page 55. Because of the nature of the Internet, some website addresses may have changed since publication. The publisher has no responsibility for any such changes or for the content of cited sources.

WHAT IS A VOLCANO?

A volcano is an opening in Earth's **crust** through which ash, gases, and **molten** rock from below ground erupt onto Earth's surface or into the **atmosphere.** The word *volcano* is also used to describe the cone-shaped mountain or hill created by accumulated ash and rock at the site of the opening.

Parts of a volcano

A typical volcano has a **cone** made up of material from past **eruptions.** Below the volcano is a **magma** *(MAG muh*) **chamber,** which contains molten rock. (Molten rock is called **magma** when it is below Earth's surface and **lava** when it is above.) The magma rises through a central tube, called a **conduit,** to an opening on the surface, called a **vent**. Magma may also emerge from **side vents.** The typical bowl-shaped depression at the top of a volcano is called a **crater**.

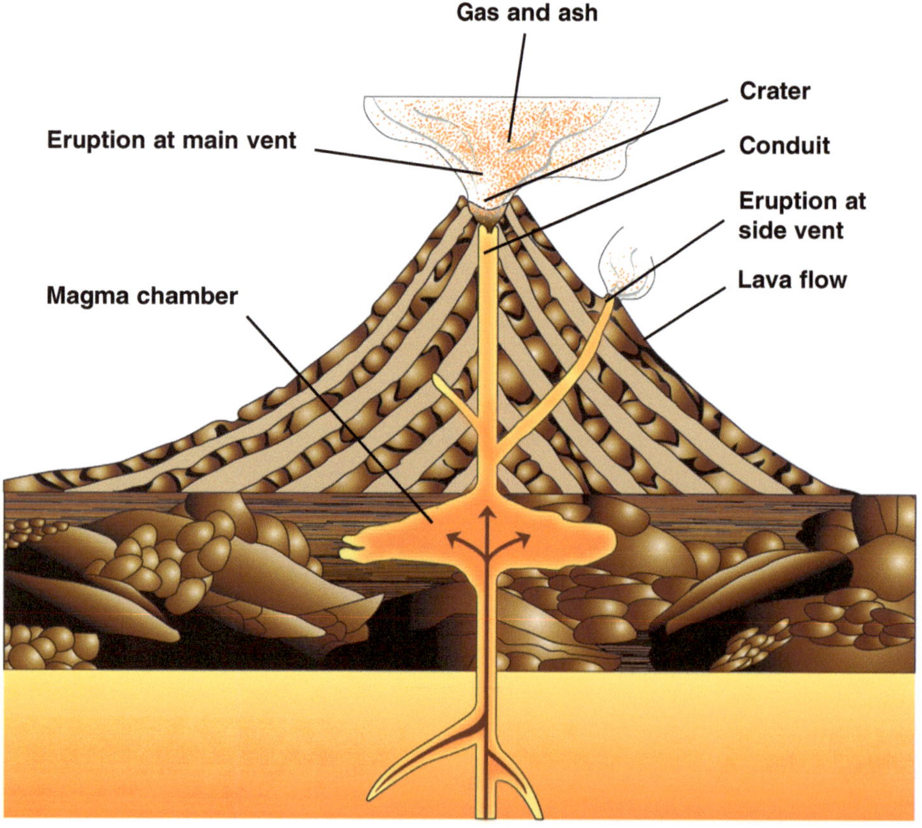

Volcanic eruptions

Some volcanoes erupt only rarely, others occasionally, and some continually. Volcanoes erupt when magma collects in giant pockets deep under the ground. Pressure inside the pockets forces the magma through the rocks above, resulting in a volcanic eruption.

Magma rises from deep underground through a conduit and other tubes to emerge from vents.

Volcanic hazards

Volcanic eruptions are one of nature's most dangerous events, and hundreds of thousands of people have died in them. Of the hazards created by a volcano, the flow of lava is usually the least dangerous. In most instances, lava moves at about 6 miles (10 kilometers) per hour, so people and animals can usually escape. Volcanoes can also eject flying rocks, called **pyroclastic** *(py ruh KLAS tihk)* **bombs.** These bombs are only somewhat more hazardous than lava flows, because they usually are limited to the area near the volcano's vent.

Far more dangerous are clouds of hot gases and ash called **pyroclastic flows**. Another term for these flows is *nuée ardente,* French for *glowing clouds.* Pyroclastic flows can choke or poison people with gases, bury them in **debris,** and burn them with temperatures up to 1100 °F (600 °C). A typical pyroclastic flow might advance at speeds of 50 to 150 miles (80 to 240 kilometers) per hour. People and animals cannot outrun pyroclastic flows. The secondary effects of volcanoes, such as **lahars** *(LAH hahrz)* and **tsunamis** *(tsoo NAH meez),* have also killed many thousands of people.

A volcano ejects a tall cloud of gas and ash—known as an eruption column.

THE WORD VOLCANO

The word *volcano* comes from the name of Vulcan, the Roman god of fire, who served as blacksmith for the gods. The ancient Romans believed that Vulcan lived on the island of Vulcano, off the southwest coast of what is now Italy. There, Vulcan made weapons for the other gods. Eruptions from the volcano on the island were said to be sparks from Vulcan's forge.

WHERE DO VOLCANOES OCCUR?

Earth consists of three main layers. The outer layer, called the **crust**, is made up of solid rock. The crust is between 5 and 25 miles (8 and 40 kilometers) thick. In general, the crust under continents is thicker than that under oceans. Beneath the crust is a thick layer of rock called the **mantle.** The mantle is about 1,800 miles (2,900 kilometers) thick. The upper portion of the mantle is solid. In the lower mantle, the rock is so hot that, though solid, it flows. At the center of Earth is the **core**. The core is about 2,200 miles (3,500 kilometers) thick.

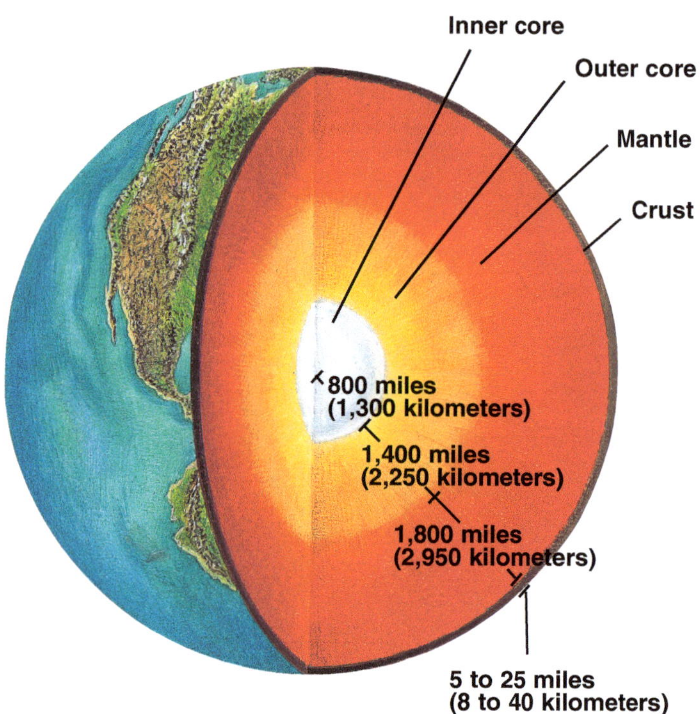

Beneath Earth's solid crust are the mantle and the outer core and inner core.

The crust and upper portion of the mantle form the **lithosphere** *(LIHTH uh sfihr).* The lower region of the mantle is called the **asthenosphere** *(as THEHN uh sfihr).* The location of many of the world's volcanoes is closely related to the activity of the **tectonic** *(tehk TON ihk)* **plates** that make up the lithosphere.

Plates and boundaries

Earth's surface consists of about 30 tectonic plates. Some of these plates are small, but others are huge. The plates rest on top of the asthenosphere. The asthenosphere flows very slowly, so the tectonic plates above move slowly as well. A typical plate slides along at just 4 inches (10 centimeters) per year.

Most volcanoes occur at the plate boundaries, the regions where plates meet. At a **divergent plate boundary,** plates move away from each other. **Magma** rises up to fill the gap between the plates. Divergent plate boundaries are located mostly on ocean floors.

At a **convergent plate boundary,** plates move toward each other.

One plate slides under the other and moves down into the asthenosphere. This process is called **subduction** *(suhb DUHK shuhn),* and the areas where it occurs are referred to as **subduction zones.** As the lower plate sinks, it carries water trapped within the rock deep into the hot mantle. The water eventually boils into the overlying mantle, causing it to melt. This produces pockets of magma that rise up through the upper plate to form volcanoes.

Hot spots

Some volcanoes are found at **hot spots**—places where an underground concentration of heat exists. This heat melts rock beneath the crust. The melted rock rises slowly to the surface, where it erupts as lava**.** Volcanoes caused by hot spots can occur far from plate boundaries, either on land or in the ocean. The volcanoes of the Hawaiian Islands, in the Pacific Ocean, are hot-spot volcanoes.

THE "RING OF FIRE"

There are subduction zones all around the edges of the Pacific Ocean, where the handful of plates that lie beneath the ocean are sinking beneath the surrounding plates. These subduction zones have created a horseshoe-shaped belt of volcanoes that stretches from New Zealand northwest to Indonesia and the Philippines, northeast to Japan, east to Alaska, and then along the west coast of the Americas to the southern tip of Chile. This belt of volcanic activity is known as the "Ring of Fire."

Volcanoes are often found near the boundaries between Earth's tectonic plates.

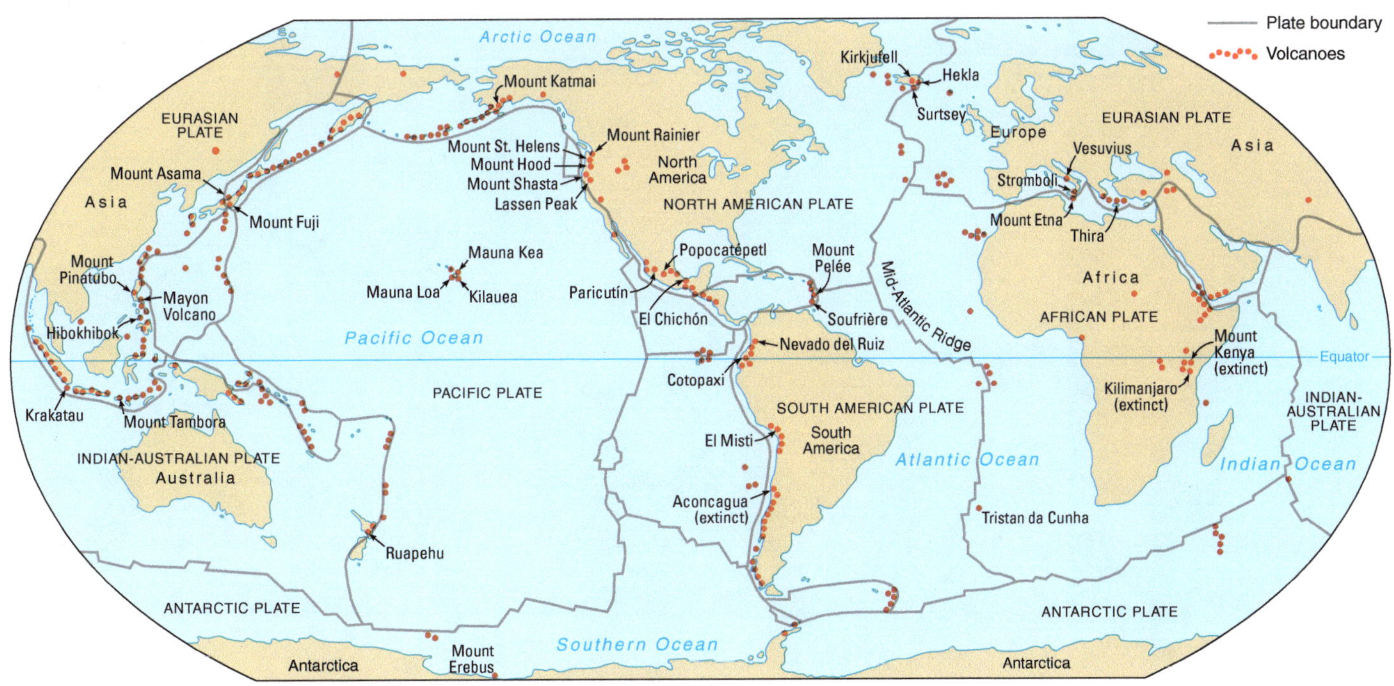

MOUNT SAINT HELENS

Mount Saint Helens is a volcano in the Cascade Mountains in the U.S. state of Washington. All the volcanoes in this area are caused by the **subduction** of the Pacific **tectonic plate** under the North American Plate. In 1980, Mount Saint Helens erupted explosively, killing 57 people.

The eruption

In the spring of 1980, small **earthquakes** were detected under Mount Saint Helens, and a bulge began to grow on the north side of the volcano as **magma** began to collect. By mid-May, the bulge had pushed upwards and outwards by about 450 feet (140 meters). On the morning of May 18, an earthquake triggered a **landslide** that caused the entire north side of the volcano's **cone** to collapse. This landslide was the largest in recorded history. More than 1,000 feet (300 meters) of the volcano's cone was destroyed, leaving a massive, horseshoe-shaped **crater.** A cloud of hot gas, ash, and rock exploded across the landscape. Instead of shooting upwards, the initial blast erupted laterally, or out from

A pyroclastic flow rushes down the slopes of Mount Saint Helens after the initial eruption.

The vast crater on Mount Saint Helens is seen from a ridge where trees were snapped off by the lateral blast of the initial eruption.

the side of the volcano. An area of 250 square miles (650 square kilometers) was turned into an ash-covered wasteland, with millions of trees flattened. The explosion also produced a column of ash 15 miles (24 kilometers) tall.

Warnings

The **volcanologists** *(vol kuh NOL uh jihstz)* who were monitoring Mount Saint Helens predicted the eruption, and local officials set up roadblocks around the danger area. Despite the warnings, some people wanted to see the eruption from a close vantage point. Charles McNerney and John Smart were about 6 miles (10 kilometers) away when the eruption occurred. They saw the mountainside collapse and a cloud racing toward them, which they later described as looking like an avalanche of black dust. They drove at speeds of up to 80 miles (130 kilometers) per hour to escape the cloud.

LUCKY ESCAPE

On the morning of May 18, a group of people were camping 14 miles (22 kilometers) north of the volcano, outside the region that had been cordoned off as the danger area. Two of them, Bruce Nelson and Sue Ruff, later described to reporters the darkness that fell as the cloud from the eruption arrived. As the blast reached them, Nelson and Ruff fell into a hole left by the root ball of a tree that had been knocked over. This saved them from the additional falling trees, but their hair was singed and their skin burned by the heat. Others in their party were not so lucky that day and did not survive.

STUDYING VOLCANOES

Volcanologists study both **active** and **dormant** volcanoes. They try to understand how and why volcanoes erupt. This knowledge helps them to predict **eruptions.** Observatories have been set up on or near major active volcanoes to monitor their activity.

Techniques and tools

Volcanologists use a range of techniques and tools to monitor volcanoes. One of their most important resources is **seismology,** the study of **earthquakes.** Small earthquakes coming from under a volcano show that rocks are breaking apart or that **magma** or gas is moving about deep under Earth's surface. Instruments called **seismometers** detect earthquakes. A network of seismometers is used to work out exactly where an earthquake happened.

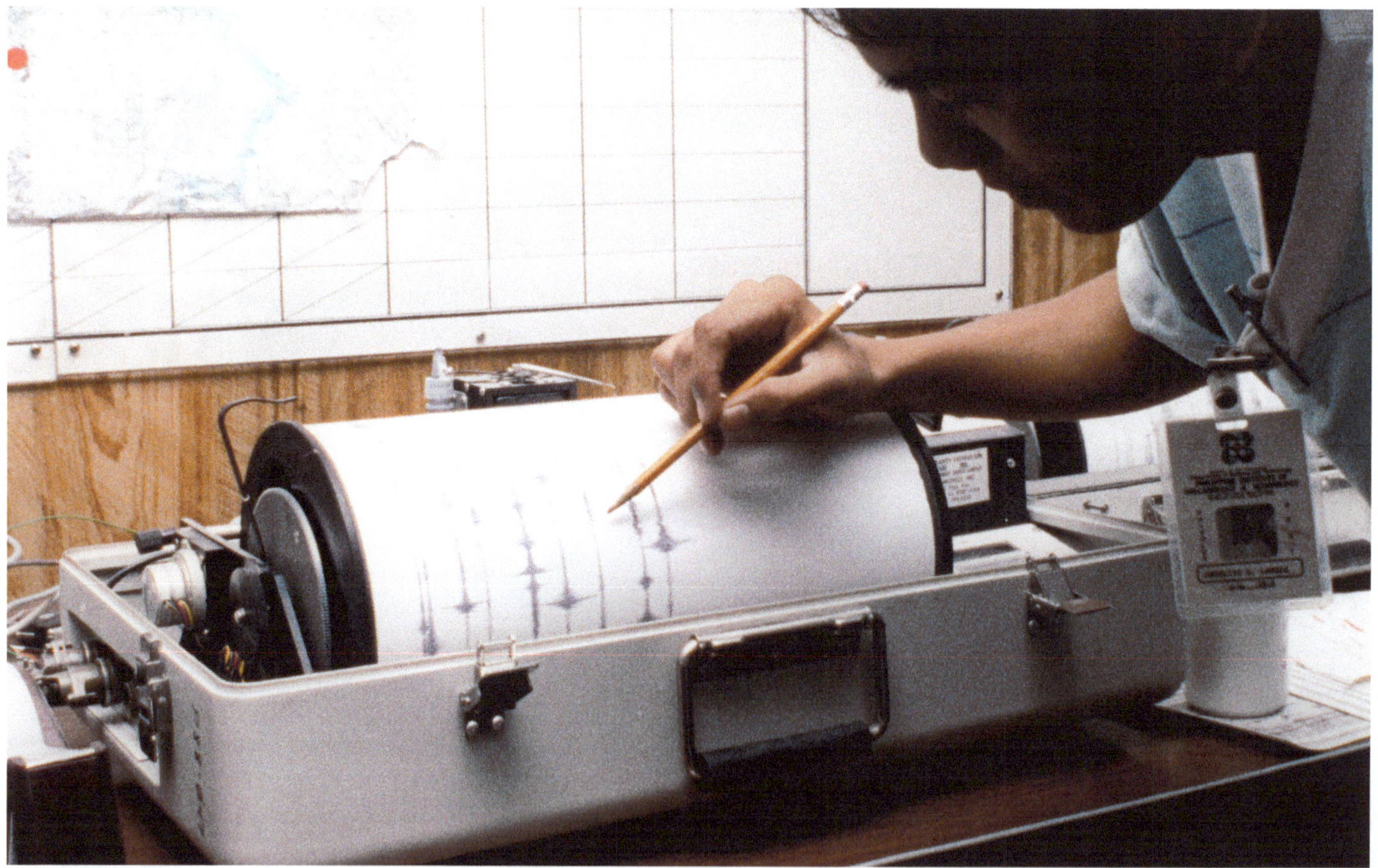

A seismometer detects and records ground motion caused by earthquakes, which may signal an impending eruption.

A volcano's top normally swells as magma pushes up from underneath, so volcanologists monitor the cone for movement. Instruments called **tiltmeters** register both upward and downward movement. Volcanologists also use the **Global Positioning System** (GPS), a highly accurate **satellite** navigation system. The GPS can be used to measure the exact position of markers placed in the ground and show whether a volcano is swelling upward or outward.

The surface of a volcano warms up as magma rises within, so volcanologists monitor the ground temperature. They measure the temperature of gases coming from **vents**. They also collect samples of the deposits surrounding a volcano and of the gases being emitted. An increase in sulfur dioxide (SO_2) in these samples could show that magma is rising.

Volcanologists take samples of deposits from the edge of a volcanic crater.

Remote sensing

Volcanologists use information collected by satellites to study volcanoes and eruptions. A satellite can measure the shape of a volcano using very accurate **radar** and can detect the surface temperature using cameras that are sensitive to heat. Cameras mounted on satellites can also photograph the spread of ash and gas from an eruption.

ERUPTION HISTORY

Many volcanoes erupt at regular intervals. The layers of ash and lava from previous eruptions can provide volcanologists with clues to what future eruptions might be like. They may also indicate which areas are at risk from **pyroclastic flows** and **lahars.** Nevertheless, volcanologists can always be surprised. Scientists observing Mount Saint Helens, for example, were not expecting the volcano to erupt in a lateral blast (see pages 8-9).

MAGMA

Magma is the name for **molten** rock inside Earth. It normally forms under the **crust,** from 30 to 120 miles (50 to 200 kilometers) below the surface. Volcanoes occur where magma pushes its way through the rocks of the crust and emerges at the surface.

Magma types

Differences in the chemical make-up of magmas can cause differences in **viscosity.** Some magmas are quite fluid, with a consistency similar to cooking oil. Other magmas are thick and sticky, similar to molasses or tar. The chemical make-up of magma generally depends upon where the magma is formed. The magma that rises at **divergent plate boundaries** is normally thin and liquid. Magma that rises from **subduction zones** is normally thick.

Magma reaches the surface at the Hawaiian volcano Kilauea, forming a lava flow.

Gas in magma

Magma also contains such gases as **water vapor,** carbon dioxide (CO_2), and sulfur dioxide (SO_2). Deep underground, extreme pressure helps keep the gases dissolved in the magma. But as the magma nears the surface, the gases form bubbles. The magma acts somewhat like a carbonated soft drink. The pressure inside the bottle keeps carbon dioxide gas dissolved in the drink mixture. When the bottle is opened, however, gas bubbles rise to the top.

Eruptions of thin, liquid magma

The violence of an eruption depends on how liquid the magma is and the amount of gas it contains. Thin, liquid magma that contains only a little gas produces relatively gentle eruptions, because the magma pours easily from the ground. Liquid magma that contains a lot of gas produces **lava fountains,** as the escaping gas flings lava into the air. Runny magma often pours down a volcano's slopes, creating **lava flows.** Eventually, the lava cools and turns solid.

Eruptions of thick magma

Thick magma with little gas produces steep **lava domes,** because the lava does not flow easily and does not get far before it cools. Thick magma with lots of gas produces violent eruptions, because the gas bubbles cannot move easily and, therefore, the bubbles blow the magma apart.

VOLCANIC NECKS

A **volcanic neck** (or volcanic plug) is a column of solidified magma that once formed the core of a volcano. It is left standing after the softer rock around it erodes away. Devils Tower, in Wyoming, in the United States, and Sugar Loaf Mountain, in Rio de Janeiro, Brazil, are famous examples of volcanic necks.

Devils Tower, in Wyoming, is a column of solidified magma that was once the core of a volcano.

VOLCANIC HAZARDS

Volcanic eruptions cause great hazards to people, buildings, roads and other structures, wildlife, forests, and crops. The direct hazards of a volcano include **lava flows** and **pyroclastic flows.** The least deadly of the direct hazards are slow-moving lava flows. However, lava flows have killed people, and they often destroy buildings and roads.

The hazards of a volcano

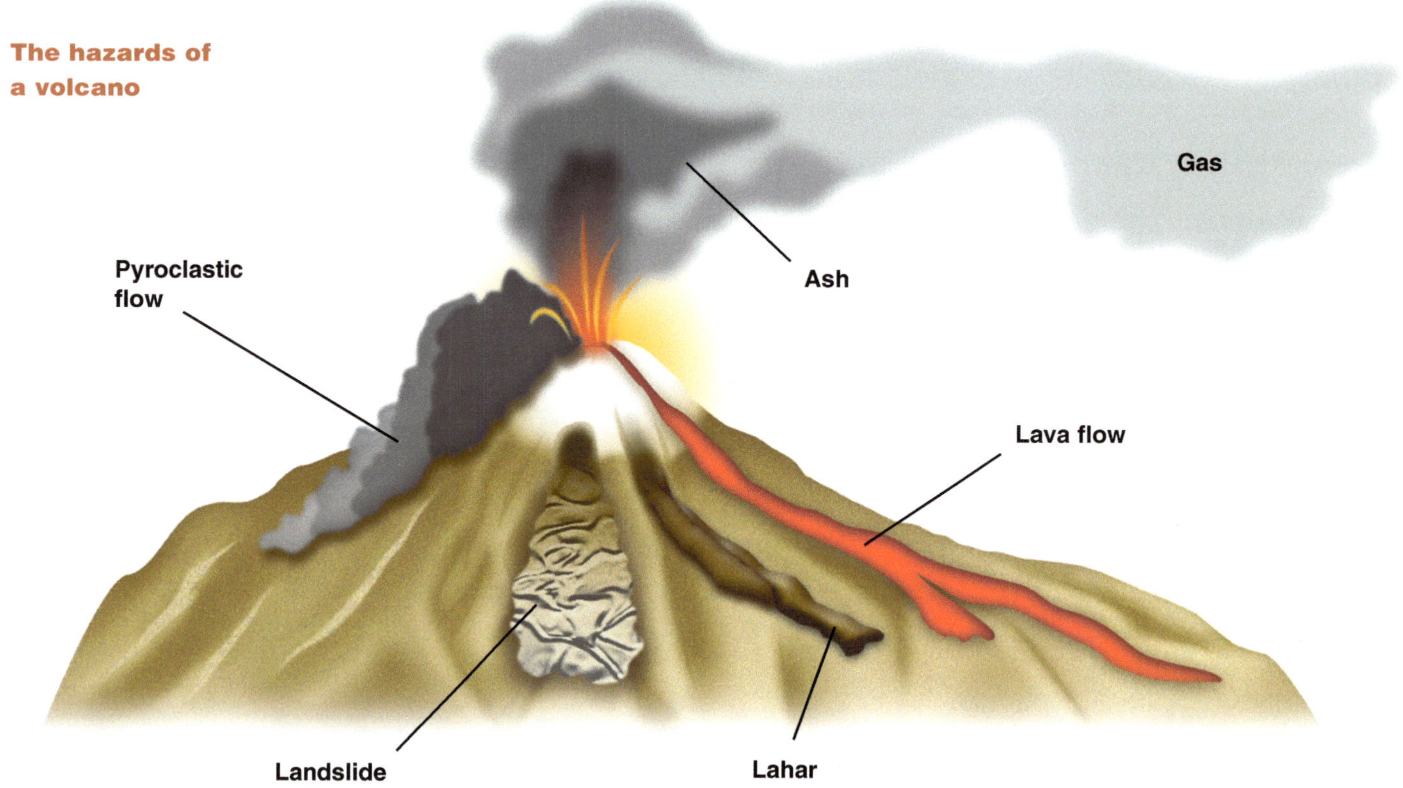

The most deadly direct volcanic hazard is a pyroclastic flow, a cloud of hot gas and ash that travels mostly along the ground (see pages 30-31). Pyroclastic flows advance tens or hundreds of feet or meters per second, destroying everything in their path. Secondary hazards that result from volcanic eruptions include giant **landslides,** high-speed **lahars**, and **tsunamis** (see pages 36-37).

Explosive eruptions

Explosive eruptions occur rarely, but they are often quite violent. Such eruptions occur when thick, gas-filled **magma** moves to the surface. The gas in the magma starts to form bubbles, and eventually the pressure of the expanding bubbles causes the magma to explode. The explosion throws gas, ash, and pieces of rock high into the air, forming a tall cloud called an **eruption column.** Explosive eruptions can also cause pyroclastic flows and lahars. Successive eruptions can build up a steep-sided, cone-shaped volcano, called a **stratovolcano,** made of layers of ash and **lava**.

Active, dormant, and extinct

Volcanologists consider any volcano that has erupted in the last 10,000 years to be **active**. An active volcano that is not erupting or not about to erupt is classified as **dormant.** A volcano that is unlikely ever to erupt again is described as **extinct.**

VOLCANIC EXPLOSIVITY

Volcanologists often rate the power of an eruption using the **Volcanic Explosivity Index** (VEI). Most eruptions have a VEI of 0 through 8, with 0 being not explosive at all and 8 ranking among the most explosive eruptions known. Mount Saint Helens had a VEI rating of 5. Each number represents around a 10-fold increase in power, so a VEI 5 eruption has 10 times the force of a VEI 4 eruption.

A lava flow on the slopes of Mount Etna, in Italy, threatens a building.

PYROCLASTS

A field of pumice on the slopes of Mount Saint Helens in Washington state. Deposits like this are often left by pyroclastic flows.

Pyroclasts, also called pyroclastics, are fragments of magma ejected by a volcanic eruption. They are pushed upward by rapidly expanding gas bubbles. **Volcanologists** classify them according to texture and size.

Volcanic ash

Volcanic ash is made up of tiny particles of solidified magma. Some particles are as small as grains of flour. Others are as big as grains of sand. Ash forms when bubbly magma is blown apart, breaking the bubble walls into tiny fragments that cool and solidify quickly.

Pumice and scoria

Chunks of frothy magma that cool and solidify before they land are known as **pumice**. Pieces of pumice are full of air pockets, making them light enough to float on water. **Scoria** is also full of air pockets but is generally much more dense than pumice. During less violent eruptions, pumice and scoria often land around the vent of a volcano. Some vents erupt only scoria, building up a **cone** of loose material called a **cinder cone.**

Spatter

Spatter is made up of blobs of magma that land before solidifying. It forms during less violent eruptions of thin, liquid magma. Spatter sometimes pools to form **lava flows** and sometimes solidifies to build up spatter cones.

Pyroclastic bombs light up the night sky during an eruption of Yasour, a stratovolcano on the Pacific island of Vanuatu.

Lapilli and bombs

Pyroclasts larger than ash, between 1⁄10 inch (2.5 millimeters) and 2½ inches (64 millimeters) in size, are known as **lapilli.** Any larger pyroclast is called a **pyroclastic bomb.** Some bombs solidify before landing. Other bombs stay liquid and spread out when they land. Yet other bombs are similar to giant, soft-centered candies. They smash open and release lava when they land.

STROMBOLI

The volcano on the island of Stromboli, Italy, has erupted nearly continuously since ancient times. It produces ash, spatter, scoria, lapilli, and bombs, which are thrown 300 to 600 feet (90 to 180 meters) above the vent. Some **ejecta** land hundreds of feet away, posing a hazard to visitors to the summit. In 1930, a major eruption on Stromboli threw pyroclastic bombs more than 1 mile (1.6 kilometers), killing six people and destroying several houses.

ASH AND ERUPTION COLUMNS

An eruption column rises from the summit of Popocatépetl, a stratovolcano in Mexico. The column from this 1993 eruption reached an altitude of 1.8 miles (3 kilometers).

Ash is created when bubbly magma explodes. The more explosive an eruption is, the more of the magma is turned into ash. The biggest eruptions make many cubic miles of ash. The ash forms clouds that stretch high into Earth's **atmosphere.**

Eruption columns

During an explosive eruption, gas rushes out of a volcano's **vent** at speeds of up to 1,000 miles (1,600 kilometers) per hour. This rush of gas sends ash high into the air. The rapid upward movement of the hot gas also draws in and heats the surrounding air. The result is a rising cloud of gases, ash, and hot air called an **eruption column.** Eruption columns have been known to reach heights of 35 miles (55 kilometers). The gas in the eruption column is lighter

AVIATION HAZARDS

Eruption columns are a hazard to aircraft because ash can clog jet engines. In 1982, a British Airways Boeing 747 flew into an eruption column at 36,000 feet (11,000 meters) over Java in Indonesia. It was night, and the pilots could not see the column. One by one, all four of the jet's engines stopped. The plane lost nearly all its **altitude** before the crew managed to restart the engines and make an emergency landing.

than the air around it, so it floats upward, carrying the ash with it. This process is called **convective rise,** and it can carry ash more than 10 miles (16 kilometers) into the atmosphere.

Ash

High-level winds carry gas and ash in the eruption column away from the volcano. Ash can travel hundreds of miles before it finally settles back to the ground. Settling ash is known as ashfall, or airfall. If the ash is still hot when it lands, it may stick together to form a type of rock called **tuff.**

Eruption columns and falling ash often block sunlight, causing almost complete darkness near an erupting volcano. The ash erupted by Mount Pinatubo in 1991 darkened the sky above the island of Luzon, in the Philippines (see pages 24–25). Ash also makes it hard to breathe. If it rains, a layer of ash just 4 inches (10 centimeters) thick can soak up enough water to become heavy enough to collapse a roof. Ash also contaminates water supplies and kills crops and other plant life.

Philippine workers wearing face protection clear ash from the streets, after the eruption of Mount Pinatubo.

PARICUTÍN

Paricutín *(pah ree koo TEEN)* is a **cinder cone** about 200 miles (320 kilometers) west of Mexico City, Mexico, near Uruapan. Paricutín does not appear very remarkable—the region is dotted with hundreds of similar **cones.** But 100 years ago, the area where the cone now stands was a flat and fertile field. The sudden appearance of Paricutín captured the popular imagination. It also provided **volcanologists** with a unique opportunity to witness the entire life cycle of a volcano, from formation to extinction.

The volcano Paricutín sprang suddenly from a farmer's field in a 1943 eruption.

A volcano is born

On Feb. 20, 1943, farmer Dionisio Pulido was clearing his field when a crack about 6 feet (2 meters) long opened in the ground. Within hours, a small **crater** formed, spewing ash and **scoria.** Pulido and his family fled to the nearby village of Paricutín, for which the volcano was later named. He recalled, "…when night began to fall, we heard noises like the surge of the sea, and red flames of fire rose into the darkened sky, some rising 800 meters [2,600 feet] or more into the air, that burst like golden marigolds, and a rain like artificial fire fell to the ground."

Erupted ash and cinders built up around the **vent.** By the end of one week, the cinder cone was 460 feet (140 meters) tall. In one year, the cone grew to 1,102 feet (336 meters).

The volcano also erupted **lava flows**

that threatened the village of Paricutín and nearby San Juan Parangaricutiro *(pah rahn gah ree coo TEE roh).* Both towns were safely evacuated before being buried by **lava** and ash.

The Michoacán-Guanajuato field

Paricutín continued to erupt from time to time until 1952. Scientists are confident that it is now **extinct.** They know that Paricutín is part of a much larger group of volcanoes called the Michoacán-Guanajuato *(mee shuh wah KAHN gwah nah HWAH toh)* field. The field covers an area of over 13,000 square miles (34,000 square kilometers) in the Mexican states of Michoacán and Guanajuato. The Michoacán-Guanajuato field is an example of a monogenetic field. *Monogenetic* means *of one origin.* In such a volcano, **magma** from a single **magma chamber** flows to the surface through different vents. Each vent forms during a single **eruption** or series of eruptions. Once a vent has stopped erupting, it rarely erupts again. Thousands of cinder cones and other volcanic structures dot the Michoacán-Guanajuato field, evidence of previous eruptions.

VOLCANIC LIGHTNING

In the eruption of Paricutín, no one was killed by lava or ash. But lightning created by the volcano killed three people. In certain eruptions, volcanic lightning can flicker within the **eruption column** or strike the ground. Scientists are not sure exactly how it forms. Ash particles in the column gain electric charges by rubbing against one another. Somehow, positive and negative charges are sorted into different areas of the column. When the difference in charge is great enough, lightning dances through the column and, sometimes, into the surrounding air and ground.

The still-erupting Paricutín looms on the horizon in this photograph taken from a nearby village in 1943.

EL CHICHÓN

El Chichón, still an active volcano, is home to a crater lake.

In 1982, the eruption of a long-quiet volcano in southeastern Mexico shocked **volcanologists** and climate scientists. El Chichón (Spanish for "The Lump"), thought to be **dormant** or **extinct,** sprang violently to life, significantly affecting Earth's climate for years.

Surprising eruption

A series of small earthquakes in the early 1980's warned of El Chichón's coming eruption. Even so, many people living in the villages scattered around its slopes felt at ease, knowing that a major eruption had not occurred in more than 600 years. The situation changed suddenly near midnight on March 29, 1982. A short, intense eruption lasting 2 to 3 hours showered these villages with ash and rocks, as a cloud of dust and gases shot 14 to 20 miles (22 to 32 kilometers) into the sky.

Explosive eruptions continued on and off until a final blast on April 4. By then, more than 2,000 people had been killed, and thousands were forced to flee their homes.

Outsized cloud

Although the damage and death toll were terrible, the eruption attracted relatively little attention from scientists at the time. The size and force of the eruption had been much less than at Mount St. Helens, the volcano in Washington state that erupted in 1980 (see pages 8-9).

Scientists soon discovered, however, that the eruption spewed a surprising amount of dust, ash, and sulfur dioxide (SO_2) gas into the stratosphere—the layer of the atmosphere that begins from 6 to 10 miles (10 to 16 kilometers) above Earth and extends upward for about 30 miles (50 kilometers). The cloud of volcanic material was spread by winds into a widening belt that surrounded Earth. By the end of the summer, a thin haze extended over all of the United States, the United Kingdom, and other countries in the Northern Hemisphere. Scientists realized this was one of the largest volcanic clouds of the century, about 20 times as massive as that which issued from Mount St. Helens.

LASTING EFFECTS

The eruption of El Chichón released huge amounts of sulfur dioxide gas into the atmosphere. There, the gas scattered and reflected sunlight, reducing it's ability to warm Earth's surface. Weather experts observed that this effect significantly cooled the Northern Hemisphere over the following year and beyond. In this way, this relatively small eruption affected more people worldwide than many larger eruptions.

El Chichón launched ash many miles or kilometers into the atmosphere.

MOUNT PINATUBO

Mount Pinatubo is a **stratovolcano** on the island of Luzon in the Philippines. It is the tallest of a chain of volcanoes in the region that form part of the Ring of Fire. In 1991, Pinatubo erupted for the first time in more than 600 years. This **eruption** was the second largest of the century.

The eruption

The first signs of volcanic activity at Pinatubo were eruptions of steam in April 1991. Emissions of gas in March and April showed that **magma** was rising. These were followed in April to early June by many small **earthquakes.** The main eruption followed on June 15. It lasted for two days and scientists calculated that it measured 6 on the **Volcanic Explosivity Index.** The eruption blew 850 feet (260 meters) of rock off the volcano, leaving a crater 1¼ miles (2 kilometers) wide. The **eruption column** was 22 miles (35 kilometers) tall, and **pyroclastic flows** reached 11 miles (18 kilometers) from the volcano, filling deep valleys with ash deposits up to 700 feet (200 meters) deep.

Pyroclastic flows and lahars produced during the 1991 eruption of Mount Pinatubo devastated the surrounding hills.

Pinatubo's effects

Pinatubo's eruption column darkened the region for weeks. Heavy rain mixed with ash lying on the ground to create

lahars. Ash deposits blocked rivers, causing flooding. Twenty million tons (18 million metric tons) of sulfur dioxide (SO_2) gas spread around the world in three weeks. It blocked heat energy from the sun, causing an average global temperature drop of 0.9 Fahrenheit (0.5 Celsius) degrees.

Human costs

Nearly 200,000 people were evacuated before the eruption, saving tens of thousands of lives. More than 200,000 were left homeless by the eruption. In all, more than 300 people died as a result of the eruption. A few died in pyroclastic flows and lahars, but most were killed when the roofs of buildings in which they had taken shelter collapsed. A tropical storm struck soon after the volcano erupted, bringing heavy rains. The rain saturated the layers of ash on roofs, causing them to collapse.

THE AETA

A minority group in the Philippines, the Aeta, made their living on the slopes of the volcano by hunting, gathering, and fishing. The Aeta worshipped Apo Namalyari, the mountain god of Pinatubo, and they considered the volcano to be the center of the universe. The 1991 eruption of Pinatubo displaced the Aeta and so fragmented them that few have returned to their traditional way of life on the volcano.

The ash-covered ruins of the village of Dolores, near Mount Pinatubo

ICELAND 2010

A plume of ash pours from Iceland's Eyjafjallajökull volcano during the May 2010 eruption in this satellite image.

The sudden **eruption** of Iceland's Eyjafjallajökull *(AYE uh fyat luh YOE kuut luh)* volcano in April 2010 was a relatively small one, with no loss of life. Yet it caused Europe's most serious transportation crisis in decades. The financial toll exacted by the remote volcano was enormous compared to the size and force of the eruption.

Small eruption...

Over a span of days beginning on April 14, Eyjafjallajökull spewed a plume of ash that rose up to 6 miles (10 kilometers) into the sky. The amount of ash produced over the course of several days was relatively small. In fact, it was less ash than some other eruptions produce in a single day. But the ash from Eyjafjallajökull rose and spread south and east across some of the most highly traveled airline routes in the world.

...with a big impact on air travel

Before it erupted, Eyjafjallajökull was covered by a giant sheet of ice called a glacier. Researchers found that the ash erupting from the volcano reacted violently with water from melting ice above the volcano. The rapid cooling of the ash made the particles shrink and fragment into fine, jagged pieces. This glassy ash, if taken into a jet engine, could erode metal, clog fuel and cooling systems, and melt to form glasslike deposits. It could also harm flight instruments, windows, lights, wings, and cabin air supply. The risk to airliners flying overhead was considered too great, and air travel over much of Europe was brought to a standstill.

Many of Europe's major airports closed on April 15, and millions of travelers were stranded worldwide. Airspace over Scotland was closed first, followed by the rest of the United Kingdom and most of Europe. Some flights were allowed to resume on April 18, and most airspace had been reopened by April 23, but the backlog of stranded travelers was huge. Another eruption of Eyjafjallajökull disrupted air travel again in early May, mostly over Spain and the Mediterranean Sea.

THE LAND OF FIRE AND ICE

Iceland, an island country in the North Atlantic Ocean, is sometimes called the Land of Fire and Ice because it has many volcanoes and massive frozen glaciers. Some volcanoes are covered by glaciers. In an eruption, rapidly melting ice can produce huge plumes of steam.

Ash from Eyjafjallajökull billows into the atmosphere, disrupting air travel across Europe.

CHILE 2011

In June and July of 2011, **eruptions** rocked the Puyehue-Cordón Caulle *(pu YAY way cor DOHN COW yay)* volcanic complex in central Chile, near the border of Argentina. The eruption bore many similarities to that of Eyjafjallajökull volcano in Iceland a little over a year earlier (see pages 26-27). Though neither eruption caused any deaths, they both significantly affected air travel.

The eruption

On June 4, after months of **earthquakes,** a new fissure opened up and began erupting in the Puyehue-Cordón Caulle volcanic complex. It was the first major eruption in the complex in more than 50 years. Chile evacuated 3,500 people from the surrounding region. Golfball-sized **pumice** fell near the Argentine border, some 13 miles (21 kilometers) from the eruption site.

Although the eruption caused no injuries or deaths, it brought significant economic harm in Chile and Argentina. The eruption ruined the tourist season for many of Argentina's ski resorts. At the

Ash from the 2011 eruption of the Puyehue-Cordón Caulle volcanic complex billows into the atmosphere. The ash cloud disrupted air traffic in the Southern Hemisphere for months.

base of the complex, heat from the eruptions raised the temperature of the Nilahue *(nee la HOO ay)* River to 113 °F (45 °C), killing millions of fish. The volcano also sickened and killed hundreds of thousands of livestock in Chile and Argentina. Many animals could not get to food or water that was buried under ash. In areas that were not completely covered, ash mixed with grasses quickly wore down the teeth of plant-eating animals, eventually resulting in starvation. The ash also contained high levels of fluoride compounds, which sickened and killed more livestock in the years following the eruption.

Volcanic lightning dances in the towering eruption column on June 5.

Air travel disruption

The eruption threw ash more than 8 miles (14 kilometers) into the **atmosphere.** The particles were especially fine, enabling the ash cloud to disrupt air travel for months. Shortly after the eruption, two airports in Buenos Aires, the Argentine capital, were closed for days. The ash then floated over the Atlantic and Indian Oceans and disrupted air travel in Australia. In two weeks, the ash cloud had circled the globe to cause flight cancellations in Chile. The cloud continued to circle around the Southern Hemisphere for the rest of the year, causing thousands of flight cancellations and delays.

PYROCLASTIC FLOWS

A **pyroclastic flow** is a cloud of hot ash, gas, and, occasionally, larger **pyroclasts.** Pyroclastic flows travel quickly over the ground and are among the most dangerous direct hazards of volcanic eruptions.

A pyroclastic flow sweeps down from the Soufrière Hills, a group of volcanic hills on the Caribbean island of Montserrat.

How pyroclastic flows form

Pyroclastic flows form in three different ways. Some form when an **eruption column** becomes too heavy to be supported by **convective rise** and collapses down the sides of a volcano. These flows are made up of gas, ash, and **pumice** and are known as pyroclastic surges. The second type of pyroclastic flow forms when steep-sided **lava domes** on the summit or sides of volcanoes collapse. These flows contain ash and larger pyroclasts and are known as block and ash flows. The third type forms when one side of a volcano collapses, allowing **magma** to blast out sideways. These flows are known as directed blasts.

How pyroclastic flows move

A pyroclastic flow moves forward because of **gravity.** The larger particles bounce along the ground, and ash swirls above. Block and ash flows often follow valleys, but flows that contain just ash can surge over ridges up to 3,000 feet (900 meters) high. Flows leave behind a layer of ash and other pyroclasts.

Pyroclastic dangers

Pyroclastic flows sweep across the landscape, flattening trees, knocking down buildings, and often killing everything in their path. Victims die from breathing in hot ash and gas, from burns, and from being buried by **debris.** People have survived pyroclastic flows, but only by being shielded from the direct blast and holding their breath until the flow has passed.

SOUFRIÈRE HILLS

In 1995, a volcanic complex began erupting on the tiny Caribbean island of Montserrat. The lava of the Soufrière Hills complex is so **viscous** that it can hardly flow. Instead, **lava domes** repeatedly build up and collapse, releasing pyroclastic flows. The flows have destroyed Montserrat's capital, Plymouth, and rendered the southern half of the island uninhabitable. Tourism to the island has collapsed, and more than half of its 13,000 residents have moved away.

The summit of El Chichón, covered by ash deposits caused by pyroclastic flows

VESUVIUS

A street in the ancient Roman city of Pompeii, was revealed by digging away pyroclastic deposits from the eruption of Mount Vesuvius. The volcano Vesuvius looms in the background.

Vesuvius overlooks the Bay of Naples on the west coast of Italy. It is the only **active** volcano on the mainland of Europe. Vesuvius has erupted many times in the past few hundred years, but its most devastating eruption was in A.D. 79, when a combination of ashfall and **pyroclastic flows** killed thousands of people.

The eruption

The eruption began on August 24. An **eruption column** grew, and over the next day 6 feet (2 meters) of hot ash and **pumice** fell around the volcano. Some people in the nearby town of Pompeii died as buildings collapsed under the weight of the ash and pumice. Then, parts of the eruption column collapsed, forming pyroclastic flows. Two flows killed most of the people in the town of Herculaneum. Another swept through Pompeii, killing about 2,000 people who had stayed through the ashfall.

In all, more than 3,500 people died. Their bodies were buried in ash, which in some places was 60 feet (18 meters) deep.

The cities were forgotten for more than 1,000 years. In the 1500's, the ruins of Pompeii were discovered by workers digging a water channel. In the 1700's, Herculaneum was discovered in digging for a well. Excavation of the area did not begin until the mid-1700's and remains only partially complete.

THE FIRST EYEWITNESS ACCOUNT

The A.D. 79 eruption of Vesuvius is the first eruption for which we have an eyewitness account. An 18-year-old Roman writer, Gaius Pliny (or Pliny the Younger), watched it from Misenum, a town 18 miles (29 kilometers) away. He described "a great cloud" above the volcano. The cloud spread over Misenum. People panicked, and Pliny fled to the fields with his mother. The next morning, everything was covered with ash. Pliny's uncle, Pliny the Elder, was also a famous writer. At the time of the eruption, he was commander of the Roman fleet at Pompeii. His ship was trapped on the shore south of the city. He died in a pyroclastic flow, but some of his crew survived. They saw "stones blackened, burned, and broken by the fire" falling on deck and "vast sheets of flame and tongues of fire" from the volcano. Today, explosive eruptions like the one at Vesuvius are known as Plinian eruptions, after Pliny.

Body casts

Excavations at Pompeii have revealed an entire ancient Roman city, including public and private buildings, forums, streets, an amphitheater, statues and wall paintings, jewelry, pottery, and tools. These items give a fascinating view into life some 2,000 years ago. One of the most interesting aspects of the excavations is casts of the victims in the throes of death. Many of the dead at Pompeii were surrounded by a liquid formed of ashes and rain. Eventually, this liquid dried and hardened around the bodies. The bodies turned to dust, leaving a cavity shaped like the body in the hardened ash. In the mid-1800's, excavators began pouring plaster into these cavities. From these human casts, we can see detailed forms of the victims of Vesuvius in their last moments.

The cast of a person killed in Pompeii. About 2,000 of the town's inhabitants were killed instantly by pyroclastic flows.

MOUNT PELÉE

Mount Pelée is a **stratovolcano** on the island of Martinique in the French West Indies. In 1902, **pyroclastic flows** from Mount Pelée destroyed the island's city, Saint Pierre, killing about 28,000 people. It was the worst volcanic disaster of the 1900's.

The eruption

Mount Pelée began to erupt on April 24 with a series of small explosions. In February 1902, the inhabitants of Saint Pierre—a colonial city known at that time as the "Paris of the West Indies"—smelled sulfurous gas and felt minor **earthquakes.** In coming days, people grew more alarmed as the intensity of volcanic activity increased. Other strange events began to occur. Large numbers of insects and snakes came down into Saint Pierre. Ashfall from the volcano apparently caused these animals to leave areas higher on the mountain. Some 50 people were killed by snakebite in the days preceding the eruption.

Visitors walk through the ruined streets of Saint Pierre after the eruption of Mount Pelée in 1902.

On May 5, part of the rim of the summit **crater** collapsed, releasing hot water from the lake in the crater. The water mixed with ash to form a **lahar** that killed 25 people. On May 6, new **magma** reached the surface, creating a **lava dome** in the crater, as well as an **eruption column.** On May 8, just before 8 a.m., the lava dome collapsed, forming a pyroclastic flow. The flow reached Saint Pierre, 4 miles (6 kilometers) away, in less than a minute, flattening the buildings and killing all but a few of the inhabitants who had not fled the island. Villages around Saint Pierre were also destroyed, along with ships in the harbor. One sailor who survived described the pyroclastic flow as a hurricane of fire. The city burned for several days, and on May 20, another flow destroyed anything that was left.

At the time, pyroclastic flows were poorly understood. Saint Pierre had not been evacuated, in part because people thought the danger would come from lava flows, which could not reach Saint Pierre. The day before Saint Pierre was hit, thousands of villagers went to the city where they believed they would be safer.

After the disaster, some parts of the city were rebuilt. Today, there is an observatory on the volcano to monitor activity and warn of future eruptions.

THE "ONLY" SURVIVOR

One of the few people in the city of Saint Pierre to survive the pyroclastic flow was a 27-year-old laborer named Ludger Sylbaris (also known as Louis-Auguste Cyparis). He escaped death while in the prison's underground dungeon. His cell had no windows, only a small grate above the door. Sylbaris later described how it suddenly became dark, and hot air and gas came in through the dungeon's air vent. The heat burned his legs, arms, and back, but he held his breath so his lungs were unharmed. He was rescued four days after the eruption. Eventually, Sylbaris joined the Barnum and Bailey circus, where he was billed, with much exaggeration, as "the only living object that survived in the silent city of death."

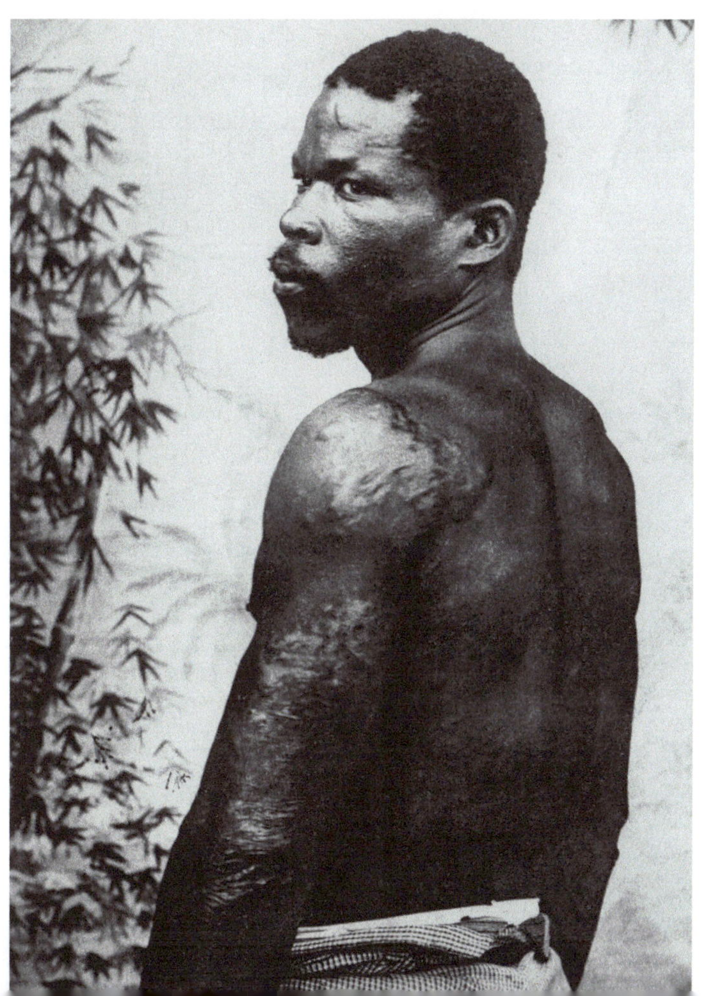

Ludger Sylbaris displays scars from the burns he received during the eruption.

LAHARS, LANDSLIDES, AND FLOODS

Mud deposited by lahars during the 1991 eruption covers the slopes of Mount Pinatubo in the Philippines.

Lahars, landslides, and floods are some of the main secondary hazards of an eruption. A volcanic lahar—a mixture of water and volcanic ash that flows down the sides of a volcano or along river valleys—is sometimes called a mudflow. Only **pyroclastic flows** are more dangerous than lahars. Eruptions can also set off landslides of volcanic **debris,** or debris avalanches, and **tsunamis.**

How lahars move

The water in lahars can come from **crater** lakes found at the tops of volcanoes, from snow and ice melted by pyroclastic flows, from thunderstorms that form inside **eruption columns,** and from any rain that falls after an eruption. Lahars can move at speeds of up to 90 miles (145 kilometers) per hour and can travel more than 100 miles (160 kilometers) from a volcano before stopping.

The effects of lahars

The mixture of water and ash in lahars is very thick and dense, like unset concrete. Fast-moving lahars carry along trees, boulders, and other debris. Lahars naturally flow down valleys, often destroying towns or villages that lie in their path. When a lahar reaches flat ground, it slows down and spreads out, covering everything with a thick, semisolid layer of mud and debris. The muddy deposits sometimes block river channels, causing floods upstream.

Tsunamis

Explosive eruptions, landslides that fall into the sea, and pyroclastic flows can cause giant wave events called tsunamis. A tsunami wave can travel across open water at hundreds of miles per hour. In the middle of seas and oceans, the wave may be only a few feet high and hardly noticeable. But as it reaches the shallow water near a coast, it slows down and becomes much taller. When a tsunami wave washes ashore, it can cause widespread destruction and flooding. In 1792, a landslide that followed an eruption of Japan's Mount Unzen created a tsunami that killed nearly 15,000 people in Shimbara City and nearby areas.

ICECAP FLOODS

Thick sheets of ice, called icecaps, cover some volcanoes. During an eruption, the intense heat melts the ice closest to the cone, causing a body of water to be trapped under the outer ice. Eventually, the water breaks through the ice, causing a sudden flood. These floods are common in Iceland, where they are known as *jökulhlaups*, which means glacier bursts.

In 1996, an icecap flood left this wide plain of mud in southern Iceland. The flood damaged the bridge in the foreground.

THE ARMERO LAHAR

The ruins of Armero, Colombia, after a giant lahar flowed through the town

On Nov. 13, 1985, the Nevado del Ruiz volcano in Colombia erupted. A subsequent **lahar** buried the town of Armero, killing more than 23,000 people and injuring 5,000 others.

The eruption

Nevado del Ruiz is a **stratovolcano**. At an elevation of over 17,000 feet (5,200 meters), the volcano's summit is always covered with snow and ice. The 1985 eruption was not very violent, but **pyroclastic flows** melted ice and snow, releasing millions of tons of water. The water mixed with ash and other rocky material to form lahars that rushed down narrow valleys on the sides of the volcano. The lahars traveled more than 60 miles (100 kilometers) from the volcano.

The town of Armero

The town of Armero was about 46 miles (74 kilometers) from Nevado del Ruiz and lay at the end of a steep-sided valley. After the eruption of the Nevado del Ruiz volcano, a series of lahars poured down the valley and spread out over the town. One wave of mud was 130 feet (40 meters) high. The flow swept away buildings, trees, people, and animals. It struck at night, when most people were in bed and had little chance of escape. Three out of four townspeople were buried alive.

A survivor's account

A taxi driver, Modesto Bocanegra Menesses, survived the destruction of Armero. He was asleep when the lahar hit. The force of the flow knocked down his house and carried him about 2 miles (3 kilometers) away. He was hit again and again by debris. "The mud grabbed me and pushed me under. I would come up again and again. I couldn't breathe," he said later. Bocanegra lost his wife, two of his three daughters, and most other members of his family in the lahar.

WARNINGS IGNORED

Armero was built on old lahars that had killed people hundreds of years ago. Local **volcanologists** warned that an eruption was on the way and lahars were likely, but there was no emergency plan. The authorities did not order an evacuation until it was too late. Instead, they told people to stay in their homes. Armero has not been rebuilt—its ruins are buried under the hardened mud.

A survivor is carried away by rescue workers. Many survivors were pulled from the mud by helicopter.

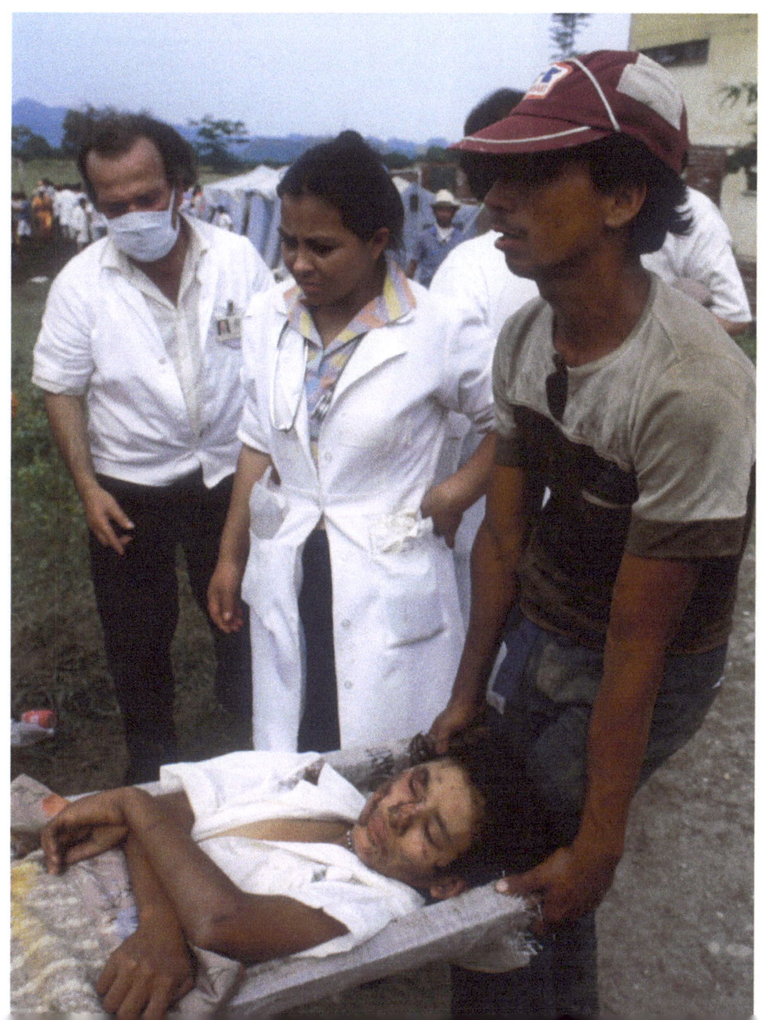

GIANT ERUPTIONS

The eruption of Mount Pinatubo in 1991 (see pages 24-25) was the second largest of the last 100 years, but it was minor compared with giant volcanic eruptions that have occurred in the past. Giant eruptions can spread ash for thousands of miles and affect the weather globally.

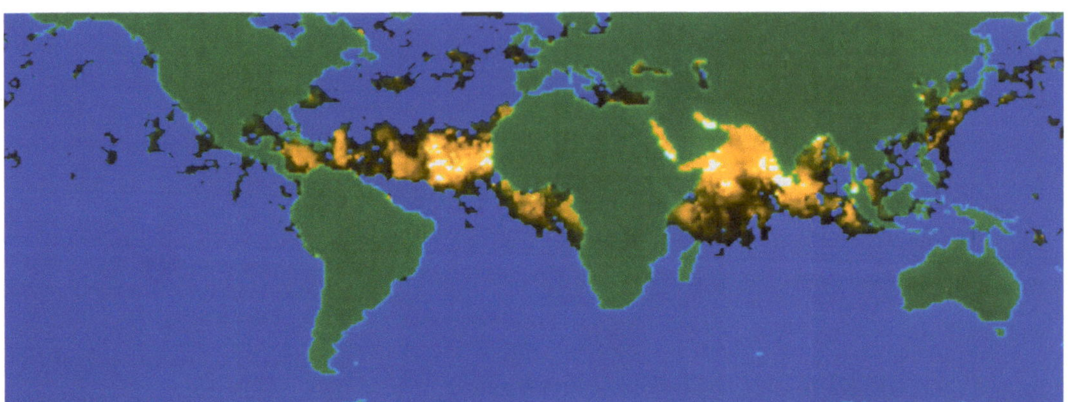

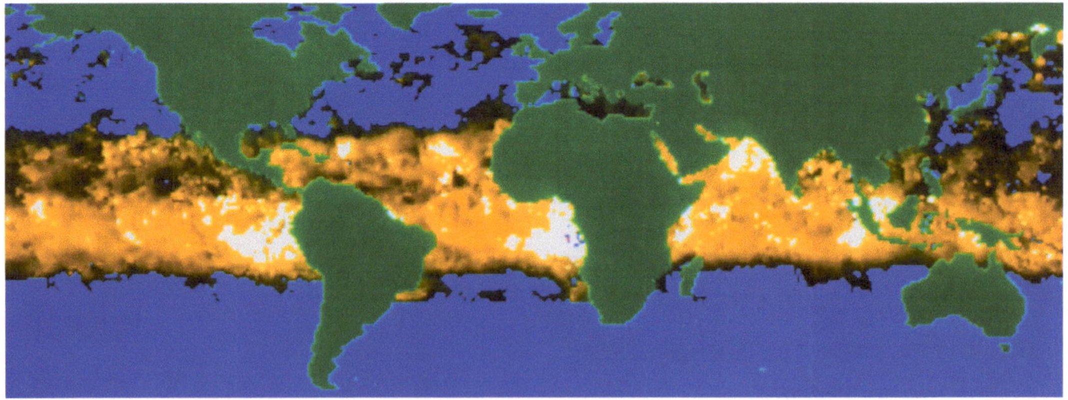

Computer-generated images show the spread of sulfur dioxide into the atmosphere soon after the eruption of Mount Pinatubo (top) and two months later (bottom). In the atmosphere, the sulfur dioxide mixes with water to form particles that block sunlight. These particles, combined with volcanic ash, cool temperatures on Earth. After Pinatubo erupted, average global temperatures dropped by about 0.9 Fahrenheit (0.5 Celsius) degrees. The eruption of the supervolcano Toba lowered temperatures up to ten times that much.

Giant calderas

A **caldera** (*kal DIHR uh*) is a huge depression, or dent, in Earth's surface formed when the ground collapses into a hole left behind by erupting **magma.** The largest calderas, sometimes called **supervolcanoes,** form where vast pools of magma collect below the surface. Magma in these volcanoes is very **viscous** and traps a lot of gases, so super-volcanoes erupt a huge amount of magma that has been under tremendous pressure. Afterward, it may take hundreds of thousands of years for such a volcano to erupt again. As the large amount of material erupts, the overlying rock collapses, forming a huge depression.

The Toba eruption

The island of Sumatra in Indonesia had a caldera volcano, named Toba, which erupted about 74,000 years ago. The eruption produced 300 times as much ash as the 1991 eruption of Mount Pinatubo and left a caldera 60 miles (100 kilometers) long and 18 miles (29 kilometers) wide. Ash piled to a depth of 4 inches (10 centimeters) at a distance of 1,900 miles (3,100 kilometers) from the eruption. **Volcanologists** calculate that the eruption measured 8 on the **Volcanic Explosivity Index.** Toba caused a drop in average global temperature of 5 to 9 Fahrenheit (3 to 5 Celsius) degrees. This fall in temperature may have killed as many as half the trees in the Northern Hemisphere.

YELLOWSTONE

There has not been an eruption of a supervolcano in modern times, and the sites of many past eruptions remain undetected. Perhaps the most well-known and most-visited supervolcano is in Yellowstone National Park in the western United States. The caldera of the Yellowstone supervolcano is about 45 miles (70 kilometers) by 30 miles (50 kilometers), forming a major portion of the park.

The formation of a caldera by the eruption of a supervolcano

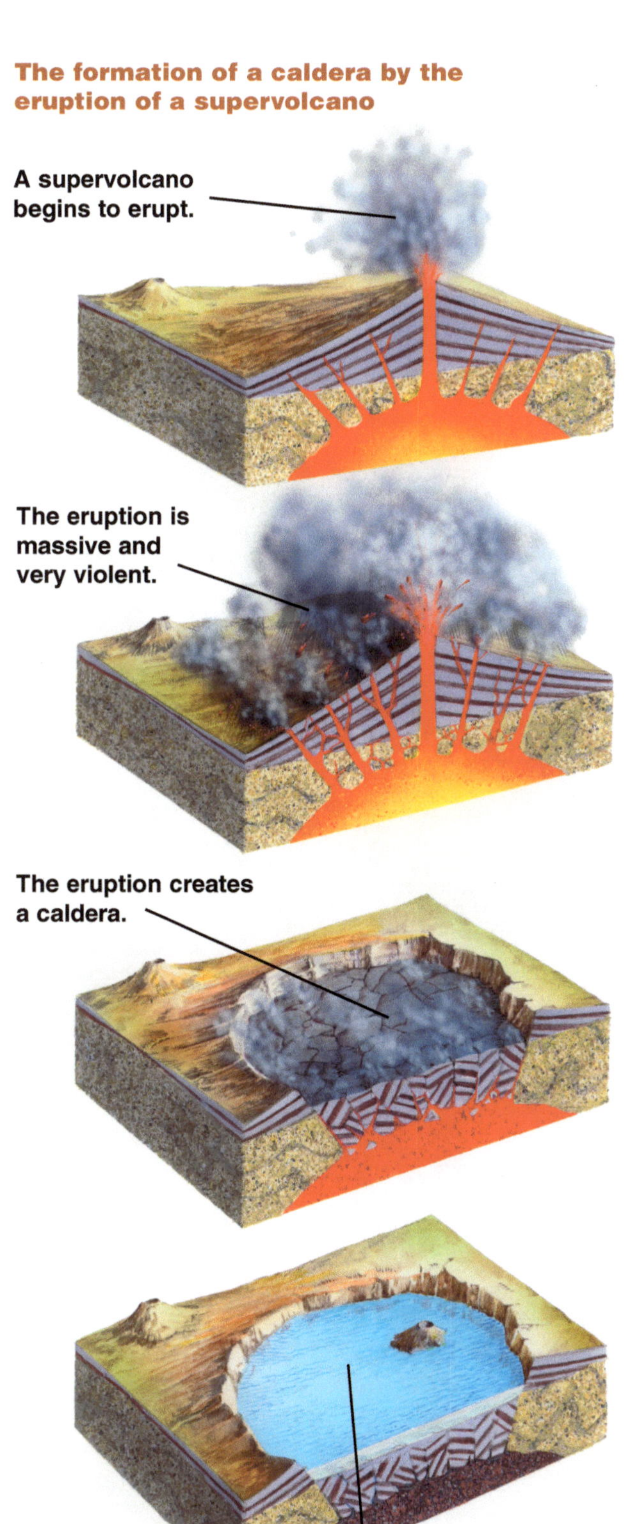

YELLOWSTONE VOLCANO OBSERVATORY

Yellowstone National Park, in the northwestern United States, is a popular tourist destination, partially because of its **active** volcanic features. There are hundreds of **geysers** and thousands of hot springs and bubbling mud pools. The park sits over one of the world's largest **caldera** complexes. **Volcanologists** at the Yellowstone Volcano Observatory monitor the caldera carefully because it is active and so may erupt again in the future.

Eruptions at Yellowstone

The Yellowstone caldera is over a **hot spot** in Earth's **crust.** The caldera formed about 640,000 years ago when the ground collapsed into a **magma chamber** after a gigantic eruption, which has been ranked as an 8 on the **Volcanic Explosivity Index.** The eruption produced 500 times as much material as the eruption of Mount Saint Helens in 1981. **Pyroclastic flows** left layers of **tuff** up to 1,300 feet (400 meters) thick, and ash from the eruption has been found nearly everywhere in what is now the United States. Two other large calderas nearby were formed by eruptions about 1.3 million years ago and 2.1 million years ago.

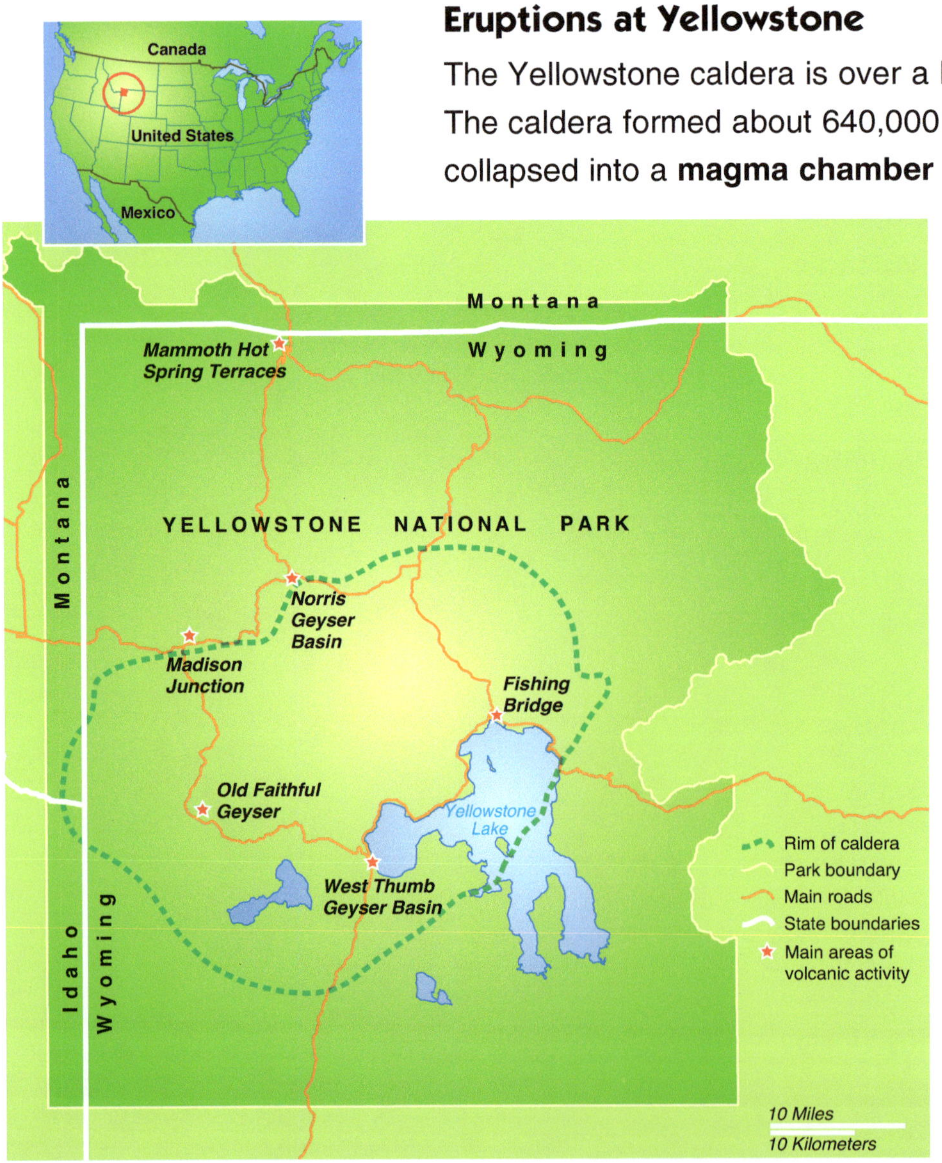

The Yellowstone caldera, created by an eruption 640,000 years ago, underlies much of Yellowstone National Park.

The observatory

The Yellowstone Volcano Observatory (YVO) was erected in 2001 to monitor volcanic activity in the Yellowstone caldera. The U.S. Geological Survey (USGS), Yellowstone National Park, and the University of Utah operate it jointly. The YVO incorporates a network of **seismometers** to monitor earthquakes and a network of **Global Positioning System** (GPS) stations to monitor ground movements. Data are sent from the networks to the University of Utah to be recorded and analyzed. Dozens of small earthquakes are detected every month, as the center of the caldera rises by about 2.5 inches (6.4 centimeters) a year, but there are no signs that another eruption will occur anytime soon. A survey using seismometers has shown a magma chamber underneath the caldera measuring 40 miles (60 kilometers) by 25 miles (40 kilometers) and 10 miles (16 kilometers) deep.

Geysers—and other places where superheated water rises to the surface—are evidence of the immense volcanic activity beneath Yellowstone's scenic terrain.

A CATASTROPHIC ERUPTION

Another event similar to the eruption 640,000 years ago would be catastrophic for North America and the world. Its effects are difficult to imagine. The amount of ash in the sky from such an event would cause the temperature of Earth to become much colder. Half of the United States could be covered in ash up to 3 feet (1 meter) deep. The disruption to agriculture in the U.S. could lead to famine and starvation globally. Human civilization would be challenged to survive. Fortunately, scientists do not think Yellowstone shows any signs of an eruption on this scale within the next few centuries.

KRAKATAU

Krakatau is one of a line of volcanoes between the islands of Sumatra and Java in Indonesia. Parts of the volcano's top form the islands of Krakatau, Anak Krakatau, Sertung (Lang), and Payang (Verlaten).

The 1883 eruption

Before the eruption, Krakatau was a huge **stratovolcano** standing 2,667 feet (813 meters) above sea level. The eruption began in May 1883, but the main eruption came on August 27. Scientists calculate that the eruption measured 6 on the **Volcanic Explosivity Index.** A series of gigantic explosions on the morning of August 27 created an **eruption column** that was probably more than 15 miles (24 kilometers) tall and huge **pyroclastic flows.** The final blast blew the island apart and was heard 3,000 miles (4,800 kilometers) away. Then, two-thirds of the island collapsed into the empty **magma chamber,** creating a **caldera** 4 miles (6 kilometers) below sea level.

The 1883 eruption of Krakatau destroyed much of the island (shaded blue). Anak Krakatau is a new island forming in the caldera of the volcano. Payang (Verlaten) and Sertung (Lang) islands are remnants of older volcanic islands.

Krakatau lies in the Sunda Strait of Indonesia, between the islands of Sumatra and Java.

Krakatau's effects

The pyroclastic flows killed several thousand people on nearby islands. The pyroclastic flows and the collapse of the volcano into the sea also caused a series of **tsunamis** up to 130 feet (40 meters) high that killed 36,000 people on the coasts of Sumatra and Java. People living up to 500 miles (800 kilometers) away were killed, and some islands close to Krakatau were completely submerged. Ash blown into the **atmosphere** caused spectacular red sunsets around the world for the next three years. Scientists estimate that 30 million tons (27 million metric tons) of sulfur dioxide (SO_2) were released, causing world temperatures to fall by up to 0.9 Fahrenheit (0.5 Celsius) degrees for the next five years.

FALL OF ATLANTIS?

A volcanic eruption often compared with that of Krakatau occurred at Thera (now called Santorini), an island in the Mediterranean Sea, near Crete. Scientists have recently determined, however, that the 1650 B.C. eruption at Santorini was actually twice as large as previously thought. New data shows that the volcano at Santorini ejected 14 cubic miles (58 cubic kilometers) of hot ash and lava. That is six times the amount of **ejecta** erupted from Krakatau. The eruption at Santorini is thought to have led to the fall of the ancient Minoan civilization. Additionally, some scientists think that the legend of the lost continent of Atlantis might not be a legend. According to some experts, the description of Atlantis, the place said to have sank beneath the waves "in a single day and night of misfortune," matches the island of Thera.

Krakatau erupts in an 1888 illustration.

MOUNT TAMBORA

Mount Tambora, on the island of Sumbawa in Indonesia, lies in the same line of **stratovolcanoes** as Krakatau. Tambora lies along the Ring of Fire, over a **subduction zone** where the Indian-Australian **tectonic plate** moves beneath the Eurasian tectonic plate. The volcano last erupted in 1815. Scientists calculate that the eruption measured 7 on the **Volcanic Explosivity Index.** It was probably one of the largest eruptions in the last 10,000 years, and it had serious long-term effects on the world's weather.

The caldera of Mount Tambora appears as a shadowy circle on the island of Sumbawa in this photograph taken from the U.S. space shuttle.

The eruption

The eruption of Mount Tambora began on April 5, 1815, when an explosion created an **eruption column** 21 miles (34 kilometers) tall. The eruption became more violent on April 15, when a new column formed 27 miles (43 kilometers) in height. Hundreds of thousands of tons of ash poured into the air every second. In all, the eruption produced 12 cubic miles (50 cubic kilometers) of ash and about 80 million tons (72 million metric tons) of sulfur dioxide (SO_2). **Pyroclastic flows** covered the island. The eruption destroyed Tambora's summit, leaving a **caldera** 4 miles (6.4 kilometers) across.

Effects

Just 26 of Sumbawa's 10,000 inhabitants survived the pyroclastic flows. People on the islands of Bali and Lombok, 100 miles (160 kilometers) away, died when their homes collapsed under the weight of ash. The ashfall also killed crops, causing a famine that killed thousands more people. Altogether, an estimated 60,000 people died.

Ash and gas from the **eruption column** spread around the world, reducing the heat reaching Earth's surface. The average global temperature fell by about 0.9 Fahrenheit (0.5 Celsius) degrees. In parts of Europe and eastern North America, the temperature fell by more than 3.0 Fahrenheit (1.7 Celsius) degrees. In North America, 1816 became known as "the year without a summer." New England had snow and frosts during the summer months, resulting in the loss of nearly all crops.

CROP FAILURES

In 1816, the crops failed because of the cold and lack of sunlight. Shortages of food led to famines and epidemics of disease in Europe and India. There were riots in France because the price of grain was so high. Many people left their homes and traveled thousands of miles to search for better living conditions.

This 1816 illustration shows severe winter weather in Brooklyn, New York, resulting from the Mount Tambora eruption.

RESCUE AND AID

Millions of people live in places where they are at risk from such volcanic hazards as ashfall, **pyroclastic flows,** and **lahars.** In many of these areas, there are official emergency plans ready to be followed during an eruption. The authorities take advice from **volcanologists** to decide whether to evacuate people. Maps of the places around a volcano that are most at risk—called hazard maps—help volcanologists to make their decisions.

Rescue

It is not always possible to evacuate everyone in advance of an eruption. After an eruption, the priority is to rescue those who have been injured or are trapped and also to evacuate survivors in case of further eruptions. These rescues occur on a massive scale, involving all branches of the emergency services and often military forces as well. Rescue efforts are often very

Ash from the 1997 eruption of the Soufrière Hills volcano led to the evacuation of the town of Salem on the island of Montserrat.

difficult—roads blocked by ashfall or lahars restrict rescuers' access and damaged communication systems hinder the coordination of emergency services. Further, ash in the air can prevent aircraft from functioning.

Shelter and aid

People who have been evacuated need temporary shelter, food, and water. Where homes have been destroyed, evacuees need long-term help. Deep ash deposits and the threat of further eruptions often mean that towns and villages have to be abandoned for good. Some of the most destructive volcanoes are in the world's less developed countries, where governments cannot cope with large-scale disasters. Farmers who lose their homes, crops, and livestock are left with nothing. In these cases, international aid is required to set up camps, to supply water and food, and to help rebuild homes and infrastructure.

A mechanical loader is used to build a dam to stop lava from reaching a town on the slopes of Mount Etna, in Italy.

VOLCANO DEFENSES

In a few places, people have built defenses against volcanic eruptions. Special dams called **sabo dams** are common in Japan and Indonesia. These dams allow lahars—especially those that occur after rainfall—to flow normally, but they block the debris carried by the lahar. Lava flows have also been diverted using barriers. Often, earthen barriers are erected to divert lava flows when their path threatens towns or structures.

FIGHTING AGAINST VOLCANOES—HEIMAEY

The island of Heimaey lies 8 miles (13 kilometers) off the south coast of Iceland. The town of Vestmannaeyjar, with a population of about 4,500, was built around the island's natural harbor and is a busy fishing port. In 1973, **lava flows** from an eruption threatened to block the harbor. The people of Vestmannaeyjar fought to stop the flow and save their livelihoods.

The eruption

On January 23, the ground split open near Vestmannaeyjar, and **lava**, ash, **scoria**, and steam began to pour out. The ground continued to open up, eventually forming a fissure (or crack) nearly 1 mile (1.6 kilometers) long. After a few days, the fissure became blocked with cooling lava, but lava continued to flow out of one main **vent.** The eruption finally stopped in early July, nearly five months later.

A curtain of lava spews from a fissure (crack) on the Icelandic island of Heimaey in 1973, threatening houses in the town of Vestmannaeyjar.

Effects of the eruption

Ash and scoria from the eruption fell on Vestmannaeyjar. Scoria and spatter formed a new **cone** 600 feet (180 meters) high on the outskirts of the town. Lava flows spread into the town and down to the sea near the harbor. About a third of Vestmannaeyjar was destroyed by lava flows, but no one was killed by the eruption itself.

Fighting the lava

Nearly all the people of Heimaey were evacuated when the eruption began. A team of volunteers tried to save homes by removing ash and scoria from roofs. They also tried to stop the lava flows from reaching the harbor by cooling them. They set up 43 pumps and 19 miles (30 kilometers) of pipes to carry seawater to the flows. In all, they sprayed 6 million tons (5 million metric tons) of water onto the lava. Some flows partly blocked the harbor entrance, but others were stopped, and the harbor was saved.

VOLCANISM IN ICELAND

Iceland stands on top of the Mid-Atlantic Ridge, which is a **divergent boundary** between two **tectonic plates.** The ridge is about 10,000 miles (16,000 kilometers) long, and **magma** pushing up from the ridge forms hundreds of undersea volcanoes. Iceland has been built up by eruptions over tens of millions of years. Heimaey was formed by an eruption about 5,000 years ago.

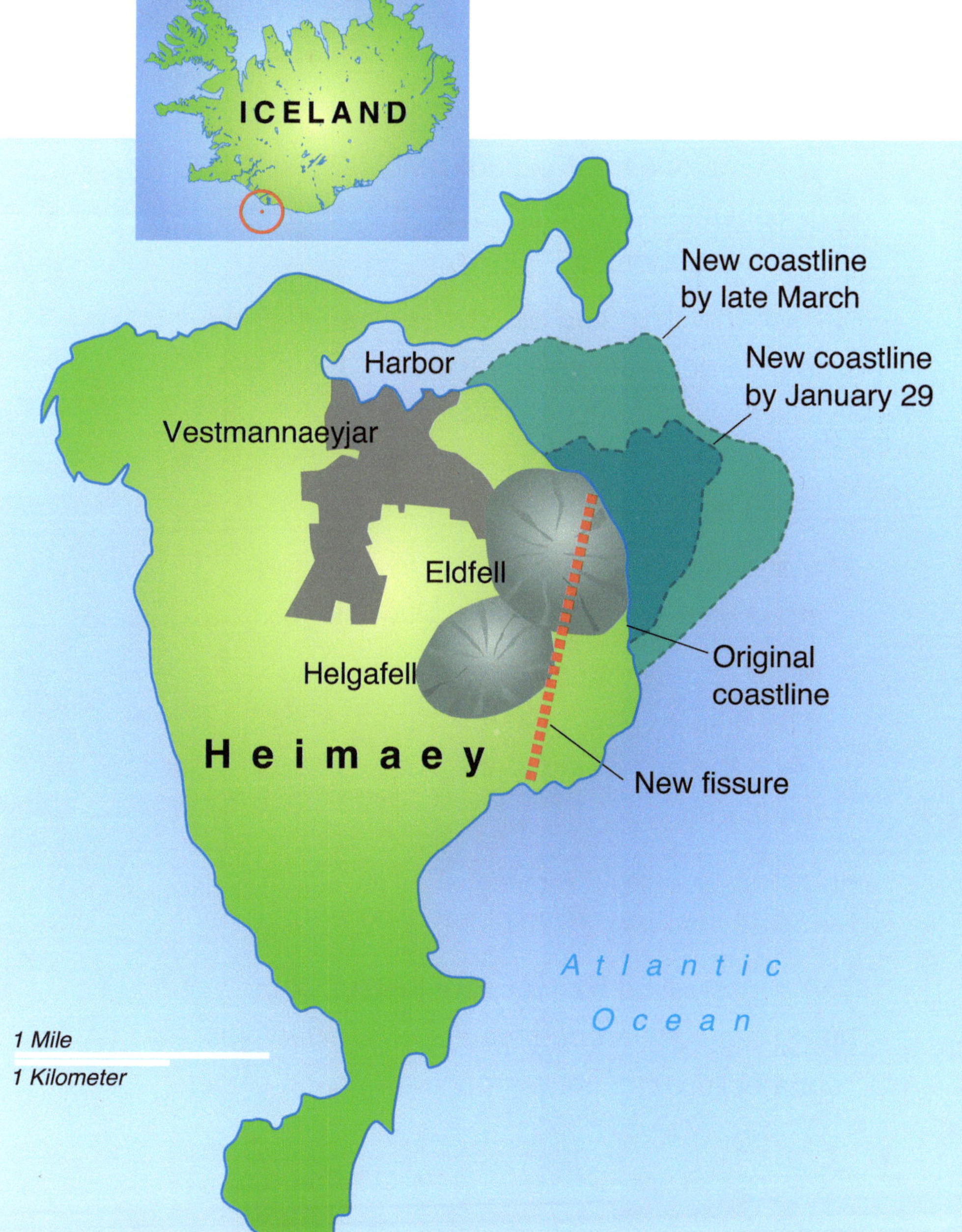

Cooled magma that erupted from a fissure on Heimaey added to the island along its northeastern coast.

ACTIVITY

A CINDER CONE

You will need

- A flexible drinking straw
- A sheet of cardboard about 12 inches (30 centimeters) by 8 inches (20 centimeters)
- A sharp pencil
- A large tray
- Granulated sugar
- Adhesive tape

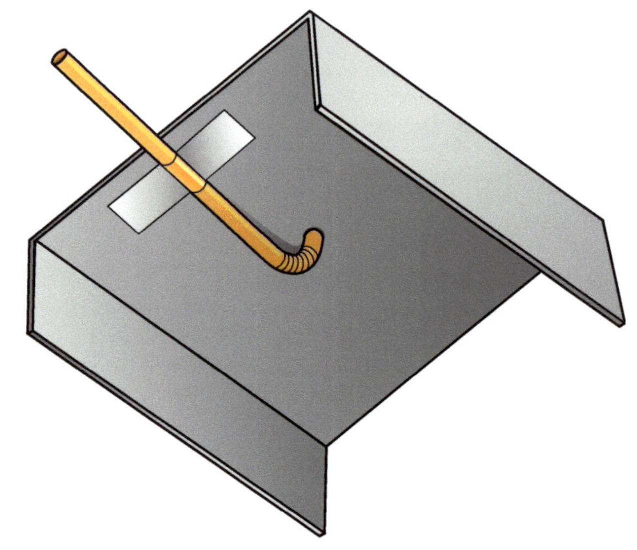

1. Using the pencil, make a hole in the center of the cardboard. Fold down about 2 inches (5 centimeters) of cardboard at each end to make supports.
2. Push the short end of the straw into the hole from underneath so that the tip of the straw is level with the top surface of the cardboard. Tape the straw in place underneath the cardboard.
3. Stand the cardboard on the tray with the straw bent so that you can blow into it.
4. Make a crease in a scrap of paper and pour a little sugar onto it. Pour the sugar down the end of the straw in the cardboard.
5. Now very carefully blow into the bottom end of the straw. Don't blow too hard.

The sugar will be blown out of the straw and will build up a cone around the tip of the straw, just as scoria builds up a cone around a volcano's vent.

active A term applied to volcanoes that have erupted in the last 10,000 years.

altitude A measure of height above Earth's surface or sea level.

asthenosphere A part of Earth's mantle formed of a layer of hot, soft rock.

atmosphere The layer of gases surrounding Earth.

caldera A huge crater or dip in the landscape formed when the ground collapses into a hole left by erupting magma.

cinder cone A type of volcanic cone that forms around a vent spurting scoria, or cinders.

conduit The central tube through which magma rises through a volcano.

cone A heap of volcanic material that forms around a vent during eruptions.

convective rise When hot volcanic gases and air rise up into the atmosphere because of their low density, forming an eruption column.

convergent plate boundary A boundary between two tectonic plates where the plates are moving toward each other.

core The center part of Earth's interior, lying below the mantle.

crater A bowl-shaped hollow in the ground caused by an explosion, an impact, or an underground collapse.

crust The solid outer layer of Earth.

debris Rubble, broken objects, and other damaged material.

divergent plate boundary A boundary between two tectonic plates wherein the plates are moving away from each other. Divergent plate boundaries are mostly on ocean floors.

dormant An active volcano that is not erupting or about to erupt.

earthquake A shaking of the ground caused by the sudden movement of underground rock.

ejecta Matter ejected, as from a volcano.

eruption The pouring out of gases, ash, lava, and rocks from a volcano.

eruption column (also called an **eruption cloud**) A tall cloud of gas and ash that has erupted from a volcano.

extinct A volcano that is unlikely to erupt again.

geyser A spring that throws up hot water with explosive force from time to time. Often, the water shoots up in great columns, cloudy with steam.

global positioning system (GPS) A navigation system in which a receiver calculates its position by detecting signals from satellites.

gravity The effect of the force of attraction that acts between objects because of their mass—that is, the amount of matter the objects have.

hot spot An underground concentration of heat that creates volcanoes.

lahar (also called a **mudflow**) A volcanic mudflow, made up of water and ash.

landslide A mass of soil and rock that slides down a slope.

lapilli Pyroclasts between 1/10 inch (2.5 millimeters) and 2.5 inches (64 millimeters) in size.

lava Molten rock that flows out of a volcano.

lava dome A steep-sided mound formed by the eruption of thick, viscous lava.

lava flow An outpouring of lava that flows over the surface of land.

lava fountain A vertical eruption of lava.

lithosphere A layer of Earth, made up of the crust and the upper region of the mantle, which forms the tectonic plates of Earth. The lithosphere is solid and rests on top of the asthenosphere.

magma Molten rock beneath Earth's surface.

magma chamber A cavity under a volcano filled with magma.

mantle The layer of rock between Earth's crust and core.

molten Melted by heat.

pumice Pieces of solidified, frothy magma that are full of air spaces, making them very light.

pyroclast A fragment of magma tossed into the air by expanding gas.

pyroclastic bomb A fragment of magmatic rock that is blown out during an eruption; pyroclastic bombs can range in size from 2½ inches (63.5 millimeters) to many feet (meters) in diameter.

pyroclastic flow A cloud of hot ash and gas that travels at great speed, mostly along the ground.

radar An electronic device for determining the distance, direction, and speed of objects by the reflection of radio waves.

sabo dam A dam designed to allow lahars to flow normally but to block the debris carried by a lahar.

satellite An object that continuously orbits Earth or some other body in space. People use artificial satellites for such tasks as collecting data.

scoria (also called cinders) Pieces of solidified magma that are full of air spaces.

seismology The study of earthquakes and other movements of Earth's crust.

seismometer An instrument for recording the direction, intensity, and duration of earthquakes or other movements of Earth's crust.

side vent An opening on the slope of a volcano, where ash, gas, and lava come out onto the surface.

spatter Blobs of magma that land before solidifying.

stratovolcano (also called a **composite cone**) A cone-shaped volcano made up of successive layers of ash and lava.

subduction When the edge of one of the tectonic plates that make up Earth's surface sinks below a neighboring plate.

subduction zone A region where one tectonic plate slides under another at a convergent plate boundary.

supervolcano A volcano that forms a huge, underground pool of thick magma. Such volcanoes then erupt, ejecting huge amounts of magma. A caldera (depression) remains when the eruption is finished. It may take hundreds of thousands of years for a volcano of this nature to erupt again.

tectonic plate One of about 30 rigid pieces making up Earth's surface.

tiltmeter An instrument that measures upward and downward movements of the ground.

tsunami A series of powerful ocean waves produced by an earthquake, landslide, volcanic eruption, or asteroid impact.

tuff A type of rock formed from layers of volcanic ash.

vent The hole in a volcano where ash, gas, and lava come out onto the surface.

viscosity A measure of the resistance of a fluid to flow.

viscous Something that is thick and sticky.

Volcanic Explosivity Index (VEI) A scale used to rate the power of an eruption. An eruption with a VEI of 0 is not explosive at all, while one with a VEI of 8 ranks among the most explosive eruptions known.

volcanic neck (also called a volcanic plug) A rock formation made up of the solidified magma from the center of an ancient volcano. The solid magma remains after erosion has stripped away the surrounding material.

volcanologist A scientist who studies volcanoes.

water vapor Water in the form of a gas.

BOOKS

Plate Tectonics, Volcanoes, and Earthquakes, by John P. Rafferty, Rosen, 2011.

Volcanoes, by Don Nardo, Morgan Reynolds, 2009.

Volcanoes, by Judith and Dennis Fradin, National Geographic Children's Books, 2007.

When Volcanoes Erupt! by Nelson Yomtov, Capstone Press, 2012.

Will It Blow? Become a Volcano Detective at Mount St. Helens, by Elizabeth Rusch, Sasquatch Books, 2007.

WEBSITES

http://science.howstuffworks.com/nature/natural-disasters/volcano.htm

https://www.theatlantic.com/photo/2013/05/soufriere-hills-volcano/100509/

http://volcanoes.usgs.gov/

http://www.cotf.edu/ete/modules/volcanoes/vmtvesuvius.html

https://volcano.si.edu/

INDEX

www.ingramcontent.com/pod-product-compliance
Lightning Source LLC
LaVergne TN
LVHW070220110826
845147LV00003B/614
9780716694885